D0090276

NINE HORSES

Nine Horses

POEMS

Billy Collins

RANDOM HOUSE

NEW YORK

Some of the poems which appear in this volume
first appeared in the following periodicals:

The American Scholar: "The Return of the Key"; *Barrow Street:*
"Rooms"; *Boulevard:* "Paris"; *Brilliant Corners:* "Air Piano" (as "And His
Sextet"); *Crazyhorse:* "As If to Demonstrate an Eclipse," "Trompe
L'Oeil"; *Cream City Review:* "Istanbul," "The Listener," "The Literary
Life"; *Crowd:* "Languor," "Roadside Flowers"; *Dominion Review:* "To My
Patron"; *DoubleTake:* "The Country," "Obituaries"; *Field:* "The Great
Walter Pater," "Velocity"; *Five Points:* "Absence," "Balsa,"
"Bodhidharma," "Lying in Bed in the Dark, I Silently Address the
Birds of Arizona"; *The Gettysburg Review:* "By a Swimming Pool
Outside Siracusa," "Creatures"; *Green Mountains Review:* "Albany";
Kenyon Review: "The Stare"; *The New Yorker:* "Earth"; *Oxford American:*
"Death in New Orleans, A Romance" "Nine Horses," "Tipping
Point"; *Ploughshares:* "The Only Day in Existence"; *Poems and Plays:*
"Bermuda"; *Poetry:* "Aimless Love," "Christmas Sparrow," "Elk River
Falls," "Litany," " 'More Than a Woman,' " "The Parade," "Study in
Orange and White," "Today," "Writing in the Afterlife"; *Poetry
New York:* "Ave Atque Vale"; *Third Coast:* "Love"; *Tight:* "Colorado";
Tin House: "Rain"

Library of Congress Cataloging-in-Publication Data
Collins, Billy.
Nine horses: poems / Billy Collins.— 1st ed.
p.   cm.
ISBN 0-375-50381-1 (acid-free paper)
I. Title.
PS3553.O47478 N45 2002
811'.54—dc21   2002024868

Random House website address: www.atrandom.com

Printed in the United States of America on acid-free paper

2 4 6 8 9 7 5 3

FIRST EDITION

Book design by Barbara M. Bachman

FOR MARY AND DANIELLE,

DEARLY DEPARTED

CONTENTS

IV.

NINE HORSES

See, then, that bronze equestrian statue. The cruel rider has kept the bit in his horse's mouth for two centuries. Unbridle him for a minute, if you please, and wash his mouth with water.

—Thomas De Quincey

Night Letter to the Reader

I get up from the tangled bed and go outside,
a bird leaving its nest,
a snail taking a holiday from its shell,

but only to stand on the lawn,
an ordinary insomniac
amid the growth systems of garden and woods.

If I were younger, I might be thinking
about something I heard at a party,
about an unusual car,

or the press of Saturday night,
but as it is, I am simply conscious,
an animal in pajamas,

sensing only the pale humidity
of the night and the slight zephyrs
that stir the tops of the trees.

The dog has followed me out
and stands a little ahead,
her nose lifted as if she were inhaling

the tall white flowers,
visible tonight in the darkened garden,
and there was something else I wanted to tell you,

something about the warm orange light
in the windows of the house,
but now I am wondering if you are even listening

and why I bother to tell you these things
that will never make a difference,
flecks of ash, tiny chips of ice.

But this is all I want to do—
tell you that up in the woods
a few night birds were calling,

the grass was cold and wet on my bare feet,
and that at one point, the moon,
looking like the top of Shakespeare's

famous forehead,
appeared, quite unexpectedly,
illuminating a band of moving clouds.

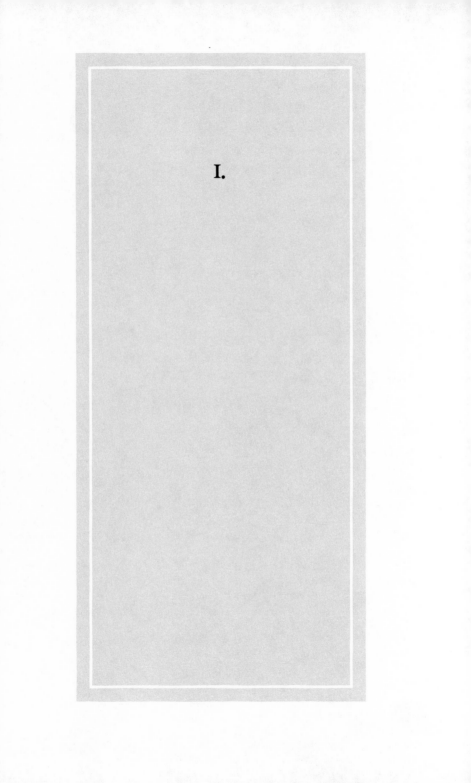

I.

The Country

I wondered about you
when you told me never to leave
a box of wooden, strike-anywhere matches
lying around the house because the mice

might get into them and start a fire.
But your face was absolutely straight
when you twisted the lid down on the round tin
where the matches, you said, are always stowed.

Who could sleep that night?
Who could whisk away the thought
of the one unlikely mouse
padding along a cold water pipe

behind the floral wallpaper
gripping a single wooden match
between the needles of his teeth?
Who could not see him rounding a corner,

the blue tip scratching against a rough-hewn beam,
the sudden flare, and the creature
for one bright, shining moment
suddenly thrust ahead of his time—

now a fire-starter, now a torchbearer
in a forgotten ritual, little brown druid
illuminating some ancient night.
Who could fail to notice,

lit up in the blazing insulation,
the tiny looks of wonderment on the faces
of his fellow mice, onetime inhabitants
of what once was your house in the country?

Velocity

In the club car that morning I had my notebook
open on my lap and my pen uncapped,
looking every inch the writer
right down to the little writer's frown on my face,

but there was nothing to write about
except life and death
and the low warning sound of the train whistle.

I did not want to write about the scenery
that was flashing past, cows spread over a pasture,
hay rolled up meticulously—
things you see once and will never see again.

But I kept my pen moving by drawing
over and over again
the face of a motorcyclist in profile—

for no reason I can think of—
a biker with sunglasses and a weak chin,
leaning forward, helmetless,
his long thin hair trailing behind him in the wind.

I also drew many lines to indicate speed,
to show the air becoming visible
as it broke over the biker's face

the way it was breaking over the face
of the locomotive that was pulling me
toward Omaha and whatever lay beyond Omaha
for me and all the other stops to make

before the time would arrive to stop for good.
We must always look at things
from the point of view of eternity,

the college theologians used to insist,
from which, I imagine, we would all
appear to have speed lines trailing behind us
as we rush along the road of the world,

as we rush down the long tunnel of time—
the biker, of course, drunk on the wind,
but also the man reading by a fire,

speed lines coming off his shoulders and his book,
and the woman standing on a beach

studying the curve of horizon,
even the child asleep on a summer night,

speed lines flying from the posters of her bed,
from the white tips of the pillowcases,
and from the edges of her perfectly motionless body.

"More Than a Woman"

Ever since I woke up today,
a song has been playing uncontrollably
in my head—a tape looping

over the spools of the brain,
a rosary in the hands of a frenetic nun,
mad fan belt of a tune.

It must have escaped from the radio
last night on the drive home
and tunneled while I slept

from my ears to the center of my cortex.
It is a song so cloying and vapid
I won't even bother mentioning the title,

but on it plays as if I were a turntable
covered with dancing children
and their spooky pantomimes,

as if everything I had ever learned
was being slowly replaced
by its slinky chords and the puffballs of its lyrics.

It played while I watered the plant
and continued when I brought in the mail
and fanned out the letters on a table.

It repeated itself when I took a walk
and watched from a bridge
brown leaves floating in the channels of a current.

In the late afternoon it seemed to fade,
but I heard it again at the restaurant
when I peered in at the lobsters

lying on the bottom of an illuminated
tank which was filled to the brim
with their copious tears.

And now at this dark window
in the middle of the night
I am beginning to think

I could be listening to music of the spheres,
the sound no one ever hears
because it has been playing forever,

only the spheres are colored pool balls,
and the music is oozing from a jukebox
whose lights I can just make out through the clouds.

Aimless Love

This morning as I walked along the lakeshore,
I fell in love with a wren
and later in the day with a mouse
the cat had dropped under the dining room table.

In the shadows of an autumn evening,
I fell for a seamstress
still at her machine in the tailor's window,
and later for a bowl of broth,
steam rising like smoke from a naval battle.

This is the best kind of love, I thought,
without recompense, without gifts,
or unkind words, without suspicion,
or silence on the telephone.

The love of the chestnut,
the jazz cap and one hand on the wheel.

No lust, no slam of the door—
the love of the miniature orange tree,
the clean white shirt, the hot evening shower,
the highway that cuts across Florida.

No waiting, no huffiness, or rancor—
just a twinge every now and then

for the wren who had built her nest
on a low branch overhanging the water
and for the dead mouse,
still dressed in its light brown suit.

But my heart is always propped up
in a field on its tripod,
ready for the next arrow.

After I carried the mouse by the tail
to a pile of leaves in the woods,
I found myself standing at the bathroom sink
gazing down affectionately at the soap,

so patient and soluble,
so at home in its pale green soap dish.
I could feel myself falling again
as I felt its turning in my wet hands
and caught the scent of lavender and stone.

Absence

This morning as low clouds
skidded over the spires of the city

I found next to a bench
in a park an ivory chess piece—

the white knight as it turned out—
and in the pigeon-ruffling wind

I wondered where all the others were,
lined up somewhere

on their red and black squares,
many of them feeling uneasy

about the saltshaker
that was taking his place,

and all of them secretly longing
for the moment

when the white horse
would reappear out of nowhere

and advance toward the board
with his distinctive motion,

stepping forward, then sideways
before advancing again—

the same move I was making him do
over and over in the sunny field of my palm.

Royal Aristocrat

My old typewriter used to make so much noise
I had to put a cushion of newspaper
beneath it late at night
so as not to wake the whole house.

Even if I closed the study door
and typed a few words at a time—
the best way to work anyway—
the clatter of keys was still so loud

that the gray and yellow bird
would wince in its cage.
Some nights I could even see the moon
frowning down through the winter trees.

That was twenty years ago,
yet as I write this with my soft lead pencil
I can still hear that distinctive sound,
like small arms fire across a border,

one burst after another
as my wife turned in her sleep.
I was a single monkey
trying to type the opening lines of my *Hamlet,*

often doing nothing more
than ironing pieces of paper in the platen
then wrinkling them into balls
to flick into the wicker basket.

Still, at least I was making noise,
adding to the great secretarial din,
that chorus of clacking and bells,
thousands of desks receding into the past.

And that was more than can be said
for the mute rooms of furniture,
the speechless salt and pepper shakers,
and the tall silent hedges surrounding the house.

Such deep silence on those nights—
just the sound of my typing
and a few stars singing a song their mother
sang when they were mere babies in the sky.

Paris

In the apartment someone gave me,
the bathroom looked out on a little garden
at the bottom of an air shaft
with a few barely sprouting trees,
ivy clinging to the white cinder blocks,
a blue metal table and a rusted chair
where, it would seem, no one had ever sat.

Every morning, a noisy bird
would flutter down between the buildings,
perch on a thin branch and yell at me
in French bird-talk
while I soaked in the tub
under the light from the pale translucent ceiling.

And while he carried on, I would lie there
in the warm soapy water
wondering what shirt I would put on that day,
what zinc-covered bar I would stand at
with my *Herald Tribune* and a cup of strong coffee.

After a lot of squawking, he would fly
back into the sky leaving only the sound
of a metal storefront being raised
or a scooter zipping by outside,

which was my signal
to stand up in the cloudy water
and reach for a towel,

time to start concentrating on which way
I would turn after I had locked the front door,
what shop signs I would see,
what bridges I would lean on
to watch the broad river undulating
like a long-playing record under the needle of my eye.

Time to stand dripping wet and wonder
about the hordes of people
I would pass in the street, mostly people
whose existence I did not believe in,
but a few whom I would glance at
and see my whole life
the way you see the ocean from the shore.

One morning after another,
I would fan myself dry with a towel
and wonder about what paintings
I would stand before that day,
looking forward to the usual—

the sumptuous reclining nudes,
the knife next to a wedge of cheese,
a landscape with pale blue mountains,
the heads and shoulders of gods
struggling with one another,
a foot crushing a snake—

but always hopeful for something new
like yesterday's white turkeys in a field
or the single stalk of asparagus on a plate
in a small gilded frame,

always ready, now that I am dressed,
to cheer the boats of the beautiful,
the boats of the strange,
as they float down the river of this momentous day.

Istanbul

It was a pleasure to enter by a side street
in the center of the city
a bathhouse said to be 300 years old,
old enough to have opened the pores of Florence Nightingale
and soaped the musical head of Franz Liszt.

And it was a pleasure to drink
cold wine by a low wood fire
before being directed to a small room in an upper gallery,
a room with a carpet and a narrow bed
where I folded my clothes into a pile
then came back down, naked
except for a gauzy striped cloth tucked around my waist.

It was an odd and eye-opening sensation
to be led by a man with close-cropped hair
and spaces between his teeth
into a steamy marble rotunda
and to lie there alone on the smooth marble
watching the droplets fall through the beams
of natural light in the high dome
and later to hear the song I sang—
"She Thinks I Still Care"—echo up into the ceiling.

I felt like the last of the sultans
when the man returned and began to scrub me—
to lather and douse me, scour and shampoo me,
and splash my drenched body
with fresh warm water scooped from a marble basin.

But it was not until he sudsed me
behind my ears and between my toes
that I felt myself filling with gratitude
the way a cloud fills with rain,
the way a glass pipe slowly fills with smoke.

In silence I thanked the man
who scrubbed the bottoms of my feet.
I thanked the history of the Turkish bath
and the long chain of bathmen standing unshaven,
arms folded, waiting for the next customer
to come through the swinging doors of frosted glass.

I thanked everyone whose job
it ever was to lay hands on the skin of strangers,
and I gave general thanks that I was lying
facedown in a warm puddle of soap
and not a warm puddle of blood
in some corner of this incomprehensible city.

As one bucket after another
of warm water was poured over my lowered head,
I stopped thinking of who and what to thank
and rode out on a boat of joy,
a blue boat of marble and soap,

rode out to the entrance of the harbor
where I raised a finger of good-bye
then felt the boat begin to rise and fall
as it met the roll of the incoming waves,
bearing my body, my clean, blessed body out to sea.

Love

The boy at the far end of the train car
kept looking behind him
as if he were afraid or expecting someone

and then she appeared in the glass door
of the forward car and he rose
and opened the door and let her in

and she entered the car carrying
a large black case
in the unmistakable shape of a cello.

She looked like an angel with a high forehead
and somber eyes and her hair
was tied up behind her neck with a black bow.

And because of all that,
he seemed a little awkward
in his happiness to see her,

whereas she was simply there,
perfectly existing as a creature
with a soft face who played the cello.

And the reason I am writing this
on the back of a manila envelope
now that they have left the train together

is to tell you that when she turned
to lift the large, delicate cello
onto the overhead rack,

I saw him looking up at her
and what she was doing
the way the eyes of saints are painted

when they are looking up at God
when he is doing something remarkable,
something that identifies him as God.

Languor

I have come back to the couch—
hands behind my head,
legs crossed at the ankles—

to resume my lifelong study
of the ceiling and its river-like crack,
its memory of a water stain,

the touch of civilization
in the rounded steps of the molding,
and the lick of time in the flaking plaster.

To move would only ruffle
the calm surface of the morning,
and disturb shadows of leaves in the windows.

And to throw open a door
would startle the fish in the pond,
maybe frighten a few birds from a hedge.

Better to stay here,
to occupy the still room of thought,
to listen to the dog breathing on the floor,

better to count my lucky coins,
or redesign my family coat of arms—
remove the plow and hive, shoo away the bee.

Obituaries

These are no pages for the young,
who are better off in one another's arms,

nor for those who just need to know
about the price of gold,
or a hurricane that is ripping up the Keys.

But eventually you may join
the crowd who turn here first to see
who has fallen in the night,
who has left a shape of air walking in their place.

Here is where the final cards are shown,
the age, the cause, the plaque of deeds,
and sometimes an odd scrap of news—
that she collected sugar bowls,
that he played solitaire without any clothes.

And all the survivors huddle at the end
under the roof of a paragraph
as if they had sidestepped the flame of death.

What better way to place a thin black frame
around the things of the morning—
the hand-painted cup,

the hemispheres of a cut orange,
the slant of sunlight on the table?

And sometimes a most peculiar pair turns up,
strange roommates lying there
side by side upon the page—
Arthur Godfrey next to Man Ray,
Ken Kesey by the side of Dale Evans.

It is enough to bring to mind an ark of death,
not the couples of the animal kingdom,
but rather pairs of men and women
ascending the gangplank two by two,

surgeon and model,
balloonist and metalworker,
an archaeologist and an authority on pain.

Arm in arm, they get on board
then join the others leaning on the rails,
all saved at last from the awful flood of life—

so many of them every day
there would have to be many arks,

an armada to ferry the dead

over the heavy waters that roll beyond the world,

and many Noahs too,

bearded and fiercely browed, vigilant up there at every prow.

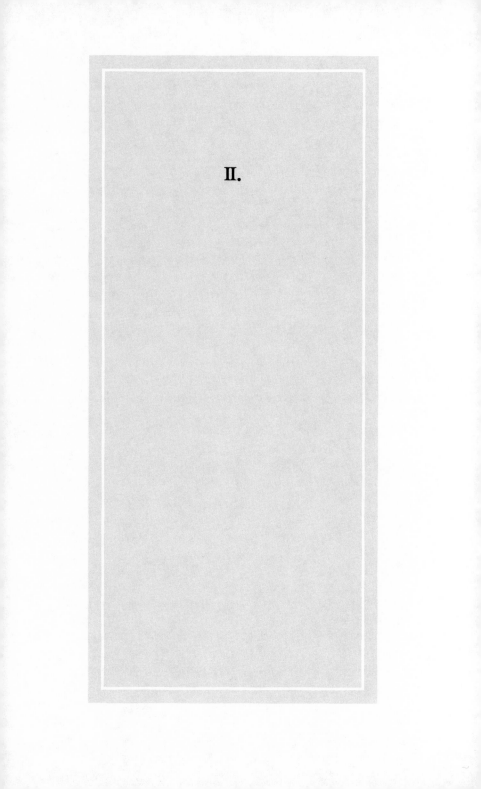

II.

Today

If ever there were a spring day so perfect,
so uplifted by a warm intermittent breeze

that it made you want to throw
open all the windows in the house

and unlatch the door to the canary's cage,
indeed, rip the little door from its jamb,

a day when the cool brick paths
and the garden bursting with peonies

seemed so etched in sunlight
that you felt like taking

a hammer to the glass paperweight
on the living room end table,

releasing the inhabitants
from their snow-covered cottage

so they could walk out,
holding hands and squinting

into this larger dome of blue and white,
well, today is just that kind of day.

Ave Atque Vale

Even though I managed to swerve around the lump
of groundhog lying on its back on the road,
he traveled with me for miles,

a quiet passenger
who passed the time looking out the window
enjoying this new view of the woods

he once hobbled around in,
sleeping all day and foraging at night,
rising sometimes to consult the wind with his snout.

Last night he must have wandered
onto the road, hoping to slip
behind the curtain of soft ferns on the other side.

I see these forms every day
and always hope the next one up ahead
is a shredded tire, a discarded brown coat,

but there they are, assuming
every imaginable pose for death's portrait.
This one I speak of, for example,

the one who rode with me for miles,
reminded me of a small Roman citizen,
with his prosperous belly,

his faint smile,
and his one stiff forearm raised
as if he were still alive, still hailing Caesar.

Roadside Flowers

These are the kind you are supposed
to stop to look at, as I do this morning,
but just long enough
so as not to carry my non-stopping
around with me all day,
a big medicine ball of neglect and disregard.

But now I seem to be carrying
my not-stopping-long-enough ball
as I walk around
the circumference of myself
and up and down the angles of the day.

Roadside flowers,
when I get back to my room
I will make it all up to you.
I will lie on my stomach and write
in a notebook how lighthearted you were,
pink and white among the weeds,

wild phlox perhaps,
or at least a cousin of that family,
a pretty one who comes to visit

every summer for two weeks without her parents,
she who unpacks her things upstairs
while I am out on the lawn

throwing the ball as high as I can,
catching it almost
every time in my two outstretched hands.

As If to Demonstrate an Eclipse

I pick an orange from a wicker basket
and place it on the table
to represent the sun.
Then down at the other end
a blue and white marble
becomes the earth
and nearby I lay the little moon of an aspirin.

I get a glass from a cabinet,
open a bottle of wine,
then I sit in a ladder-back chair,
a benevolent god presiding
over a miniature creation myth,

and I begin to sing
a homemade canticle of thanks
for this perfect little arrangement,
for not making the earth too hot or cold
not making it spin too fast or slow

so that the grove of orange trees
and the owl become possible,
not to mention the rolling wave,
the play of clouds, geese in flight,
and the Z of lightning on a dark lake.

Then I fill my glass again
and give thanks for the trout,
the oak, and the yellow feather,

singing the room full of shadows,
as sun and earth and moon
circle one another in their impeccable orbits
and I get more and more cockeyed with gratitude.

Trompe L'Oeil

It was one thing to notice
that behind the pepper mill on your kitchen counter
there was an identical pepper mill
painted on the white tiles,
and that behind the saltshaker
and the bottles of oil and vinegar
exact images of themselves
had also been applied there to fool the eye.

But it was another thing—
a higher note in the opera of Art and Life—
to see that the bundle of asparagus
you brought home for dinner,
bound with a red rubber band,
upright in a ceramic bowl of water,
stood before its own painted version,
a meticulous, Platonic rendition of itself.

I kept you company in the kitchen,
drank a little wine while you chopped and stirred,
watched you loosen the bundle
then trim and cook the stalks
while the flat, timeless, inedible
likeness of asparagus lingered on the wall.

We had crostini that night,
portobello mushrooms, grilled salmon,
and, of course, buttery asparagus.
And as I ate each spear,
I kept one eye on the portrait of asparagus—
the memory and ghost of the vegetable,
a thing beyond our devouring.

Even after I shut the door to the guest room
and fell into the soft bed,
I thought about the double serving of asparagus
offered up by you,
one for the eye and one for the tongue.

As I lay in the heavy darkness,
I felt like David Hume or William James
contemplating the nature of asparagus,
its troublesome epistemology—
the appearance of its ferns and fibrous stalks,
the reality of its succulent green tips.

Creatures

Hamlet noticed them in the shapes of clouds,
but I saw them in the furniture of childhood,
creatures trapped under surfaces of wood,

one submerged in a polished sideboard,
one frowning from a chair-back,
another howling from my mother's silent bureau,
locked in the grain of maple, frozen in oak.

I would see these presences, too,
in a swirling pattern of wallpaper
or in the various greens of a porcelain lamp,
each looking so melancholy, so damned,
some peering out at me as if they knew
all the secrets of a secretive boy.

Many times I would be daydreaming
on the carpet and one would appear next to me,
the oversize nose, the hollow look.

So you will understand my reaction
this morning at the beach
when you opened your hand to show me
a stone you had picked up from the shoreline.

"Do you see the face?" you asked
as the cold surf circled our bare ankles.
"There's the eye and the line of the mouth,
like it's grimacing, like it's in pain."

"Well, maybe that's because it has a fissure
running down the length of its forehead
not to mention a kind of twisted beak," I said,

taking the thing from you and flinging it out
over the sparkle of blue waves
so it could live out its freakish existence
on the dark bottom of the sea

and stop bothering innocent beachgoers like us,
stop ruining everyone's summer.

Tipping Point

At home, the jazz station plays all day,
so sometimes it becomes indistinct,
like the sound of rain,
birds in the background, the surf of traffic.

But today I heard a voice announce
that Eric Dolphy, 36 when he died,
has now been dead for 36 years.

I wonder—
did anyone sense something
when another Eric Dolphy lifetime
was added to the span of his life,

when we all took another
full Dolphy step forward in time,
flipped over the Eric Dolphy yardstick once again?

It would have been so subtle—
like the sensation you might feel
as you passed through the moment

at the exact center of your life
or as you crossed the equator at night in a boat.

I never gave it another thought,
but could that have been the little shift
I sensed a while ago
as I walked down in the rain to get the mail?

Birthday

Before it was over
I took out a pencil and a notepad
and figured out roughly what was left—
a small box of Octobers, a handful of Aprils,

little time to waste reading a large novel
on the couch every evening,
a few candles flaming in the corners of the room.
A fishbowl of Mondays, a row of Fridays—

yet I cannot come up with anything
better than to strike a match,
settle in under a light blanket,
and open to the first sentence of *Clarissa*.

Look at me setting off on this long journey
through ink and tears,
through secrecy and distress,
anticipation and swordplay.

As the darkness thickens
and the morning glory puts down its trumpet,
as worms begin to sing in the garden,
and Christ looks down from the wall,

I will begin inching toward the end—
page one thousand five hundred and thirty-three
in this paperback Penguin edition,
introduction and notes by one Angus Ross.

Albany

As I sat on the sunny side of train #241
looking out the window at the Hudson River,
topped with a riot of ice,

it appeared to the untrained eye
that the train was whizzing north along the rails
that link New York City and Niagara Falls.

But as the winter light glared
off the white river and the snowy fields,
I knew that I was as motionless as a man on a couch

and that the things I was gazing at—
with affection, I should add—
were really the ones that were doing the moving,

running as fast as they could
on their invisible legs
in the opposite direction of the train.

The rocky ledges and trees,
blue oil drums and duck blinds,
water towers and flashing puddles

were dashing forever from my view,
launching themselves from the twigs
of the moment into the open sky of the past.

How unfair of them, it struck me,
as they persisted in their flight—
evergreens and electrical towers,

the swing set, a slanted fence,
a tractor abandoned in a field—
how unkind of them to flee from me,

to forsake an admirer such as myself,
a devotee of things—
their biggest fan, you might say.

Had I not taken a hound's interest in this world,
tipped my hat to the first magpie,
shouted up to the passing geese?

Had I not stopped enough times along the way
to stare diligently
into the eye of a roadside flower?

Still, as I sat there between stations
on the absolutely stationary train
somewhere below Albany,

I was unable to hide my wonderment
at the uniformity of their purpose,
at the kangaroo-like sprightliness of their exits.

I pressed my face against the glass
as if I were leaning on the window
of a vast store devoted to the purveyance of speed.

The club car would open in fifteen minutes,
came the announcement
just as a trestle bridge went flying by.

Study in Orange and White

I knew James Whistler was part of the Paris scene—
the café awning and the wicker chair—
but I was surprised when I discovered the painting
of his mother among all the colored dots
and jumpy brushstrokes
of the French Impressionists at the Musée d'Orsay.

And I was even more surprised
after a period of benevolent staring
to notice how the stark profile of that woman,
fixed forever in her chair,
began to resemble my own ancient mother
now fixed forever in the earth, the stars, the air.

I figured Whistler titled the painting
Arrangement in Gray and Black
instead of what everyone else calls it
to show he was part of the Paris scene,
but when I strolled along the riverbank,
after my museum tour,
I imagined how the woman's heart
could have broken
by being demoted from mother
to mere arrangement, a composition without color.

The summer couples leaned into each other
along the quay, and the wide boats
teeming with spectators slid up and down the Seine,
their watery reflections
lapping under the stone bridges,
and I thought to myself:
how fatuous, how off base of Whistler.

Like Botticelli calling *The Birth of Venus*
"Composition in Blue, Ocher, Green, and Pink,"
or the other way around,
like Rothko labeling one of his sandwiches of color
"Fishing Boats Leaving Falmouth Harbor at Dawn."

Or—as I scanned the menu at the café
where I had come to rest—
it would be like painting something droll,
say, a chef being roasted on a blazing spit
before an audience of ducks
and calling it "Study in Orange and White."

By that time, though, a waiter had appeared
with Pernod and a pitcher of water,
and so I sat thinking of nothing—

just watching the women and men
who were passing by,
mothers and sons walking their fragile dogs—
and of course, about myself,
a kind of composition in blue and khaki,
and, once I had poured
some water into the glass of anise—milky green.

Rooms

After three days of steady, inconsolable rain,
I walk through the rooms of the house
wondering which would be best to die in.

The study is an obvious choice
with its thick carpet and soothing paint,
its overstuffed chair preferable
to a doll-like tumble down the basement stairs.

And the kitchen has a certain appeal—
it seems he was boiling water for tea,
the inspector will offer, holding up the melted kettle.

Then there is the dining room,
just the place to end up facedown
at one end of its long table in a half-written letter

or the bedroom with its mix of sex and sleep,
upright against the headboard,
a book having slipped to the floor—
make it *Mrs. Dalloway,* which I have yet to read.

Dead on the carpet, dead on the tiles,
dead on the stone cold floor—

it's starting to sound like a ballad
sung in a pub by a man with a coal red face.

It's all the fault of the freezing rain
which is flicking against the windows,
but when it finally lets up
and gives way to broken clouds and a warm breeze,
when the trees stand dripping in the light,

I will quit these dark, angular rooms
and drive along a country road
into the larger rooms of the world,
so vast and speckled, so full of ink and sorrow—

a road that cuts through bare woods
and tangles of red and yellow bittersweet
these late November days.

And maybe under the fallen wayside leaves
there is hidden a nest of mice,
each one no bigger than a thumb,
a thumb with closed eyes,
a thumb with whiskers and a tail,
each one contemplating the sweetness of grass
and the startling brevity of life.

Nine Horses

For my birthday,
my wife gave me nine horse heads,
ghostly photographs on squares of black marble,
nine squares set in one large square,
a thing so heavy that the artist himself
volunteered to hang it
from a wood beam against a white stone wall.

Pale heads of horses in profile
as if a flashcube had caught them walking in the night.

Pale horse heads
that overlook my reading chair,
the eyes so hollow they must be weeping,

the mouths so agape they could be dead—
the photographer standing over them
on a floor of straw, his black car parked by the stable door.

Nine white horses,
or one horse the camera has multiplied by nine.

It hardly matters, such sadness is gathered here
in their long white faces
so far from the pasture and the cube of sugar—
the face of St. Bartholomew, the face of St. Agnes.

Odd team of horses,
pulling nothing,
look down on these daily proceedings.

Look down upon this table and these glasses,
the furled napkins,
the evening wedding of the knife and fork.

Look down like a nine-headed god
and give us a sign of your displeasure
or your gentle forbearance
so that we may rejoice in the error of our ways.

Look down on this ring
of candles flickering under your pale heads.

Let your suffering eyes
and your anonymous deaths
be the bridle that keeps us from straying from each other

be the cinch that fastens us to the belly of each day

as it gallops away, hooves sparking into the night.

III.

Litany

You are the bread and the knife,
The crystal goblet and the wine.

Jacques Crickillon

You are the bread and the knife,
the crystal goblet and the wine.
You are the dew on the morning grass,
and the burning wheel of the sun.
You are the white apron of the baker
and the marsh birds suddenly in flight.

However, you are not the wind in the orchard,
the plums on the counter,
or the house of cards.
And you are certainly not the pine-scented air.
There is no way you are the pine-scented air.

It is possible that you are the fish under the bridge,
maybe even the pigeon on the general's head,
but you are not even close
to being the field of cornflowers at dusk.

And a quick look in the mirror will show
that you are neither the boots in the corner
nor the boat asleep in its boathouse.

It might interest you to know,
speaking of the plentiful imagery of the world,
that I am the sound of rain on the roof.

I also happen to be the shooting star,
the evening paper blowing down an alley,
and the basket of chestnuts on the kitchen table.

I am also the moon in the trees
and the blind woman's teacup.
But don't worry, I am not the bread and the knife.
You are still the bread and the knife.
You will always be the bread and the knife,
not to mention the crystal goblet and—somehow—
    the wine.

The Return of the Key

It was a drowsy summer afternoon,
hot wind stirring the papers in the room,
smoke slanting up from my cigarette
as from a tiny factory that produced only smoke.

I was reading William Carlos Williams,
growing weary of the note on the kitchen table
and the broken glass on the roadside,
so I reached into one of his small poems

and lifted out a tiny key
lying on a glass tray next to a glass tumbler
in a room of an inn where someone stood
in the doorway holding a suitcase.

I knew all things come in threes,
so I was not discouraged when the key
did not open the golden lock
on my daughter's diary,

or the empty strongbox under the bed,
and I knew I was getting warm
when I entered the orangerie
and stood before the birdcage on its metal stand.

Small wonder that the bird
fluttered into the air
and circled the chandelier
as soon as the little door swung open.

Smaller wonder
that it banked sharply
against a background of windows,
then dove and disappeared

into the anthology of American poetry
that lay open on the table—
the key clenched in its beak,
the pages lifting like many wings in the breeze.

The Listener

I cannot see you a thousand miles from here,
but I can hear you
whenever you cough in your bedroom
or when you set down
your wineglass on a granite counter.

This afternoon
I even heard scissors moving
at the tips of your hair
and the dark snips falling
onto a marble floor.

I keep the jazz
on the radio turned off.
I walk across the floor softly,
eyes closed,
the windows in the house shut tight.

I hear a motor on the road in front,
a plane humming overhead,
someone hammering,
then there is nothing
but the white stone building of silence.

You must be asleep
for it to be this quiet,
so I will sit and wait
for the rustle of your blanket
or a noise from your dream.

Meanwhile, I will listen to the ant bearing
a dead comrade
across these floorboards—
the noble sounds
of his tread and his low keening.

The Literary Life

I woke up this morning,
as the blues singers like to boast,
and the first thing to enter my mind,
as the dog was licking my face, was Coventry Patmore.

Who *was* Coventry Patmore?
I wondered, as I rose
and set out on my journey to the encyclopedia
passing some children and a bottle cap on the way.

Everything seemed more life-size than usual.
Light in the shape of windows
hung on the walls next to the paintings
of birds and horses, flowers and fish.

Coventry Patmore,
I'm coming to get you, I hissed,
as I entered the library like a man stepping
into a freight elevator of science and wisdom.

How many things have I looked up
in a lifetime of looking things up?
I wondered, as I set the book on the piano
and began turning its large, weightless pages.

How would the world look
if all of its things were neatly arranged
in alphabetical order? I wondered,
as I found the *P* section and began zeroing in.

How long before I would forget Coventry Patmore's
dates and the title of his long poem
on the sanctity of married love?
I asked myself as I closed the door to that room

and stood for a moment in the kitchen,
taking in the silvery toaster, the bowl of lemons,
and the white cat, looking as if
he had just finished his autobiography.

The Great Walter Pater

In the middle of the formal gardens,
laid out with fastidious symmetry
behind the gray stone château,
right at the center
where all the gravel paths lead the eye,
at the point where all the hedges
and the vivid flower beds converge,
is a small rectangular pond with a flagstone edge,
and in the center of that pond is a statue
of a naked boy holding a jar on one shoulder,
and from the mouth of that jar
a fine stream of water issues forth night and day.

I never for a minute wanted
to be a nightingale or a skylark
or a figure immobilized on the slope of an urn,
but when the dogs of trouble
have me running down a dark winding alley,
I would not mind being that boy—

or, if that is not possible,
I would choose, like the great Walter Pater,
to be one of the large, orange carp
that live under the surface of that pond,

swimming back and forth all summer long
in the watery glitter of sinking coins,
resting all winter, barely moving
under a smooth, translucent sheet of ice.

By a Swimming Pool Outside Siracusa

All afternoon I have been struggling
to communicate in Italian
with Roberto and Giuseppe who have begun
to resemble the two male characters
in my *Italian for Beginners,*
the ones always shopping, eating,
or inquiring about the times of trains.

Now I can feel my English slipping away,
like chlorinated water through my fingers.

I have made important pronouncements
in this remote limestone valley
with its trickle of a river.
I stated that it seems hotter
today even than it was yesterday
and that swimming is very good for you,
very beneficial, you might say.
I also posed burning questions
about the hours of the archaeological museum
and the location of the local necropolis.

But now I am alone in the evening light
which has softened the white cliffs,

and I have had a little gin in a glass with ice
which has softened my mood or—
how would you say in English—
has allowed my thoughts to traverse my brain
with greater gentleness, shall we say,

or, to put it less literally,
this drink has extended permission
to my mind to feel—what's the word?—
a friendship with the vast sky
which is very—give me a minute—very blue
but with much great paleness
at this special time of day, or as we say in America, now.

Bermuda

When we walk down the bleached-out wooden stairs
to the beach and lie on our backs
on the blue and white chaises
near the edge of the water
on this dot in the atlas,
this single button on the blazer of the sea,
we come about as close
as a man and a woman can
to doing nothing.

All morning long we watch the clouds
roll overhead
or close our eyes and do the lazy
back-and-forth of talk,
our voices flattened by the drone of surf,
our words tumbling oddly in the wind.

It's Good Friday here, hundreds of miles
from any mass of land,
thousands from Calvary.
Wild hibiscus twists along the roadsides,
the yellow-breasted bird sings its name,
and all the stores are closed
because today is the day to make hot cross buns

and fly kites from the beaches—
to eat the sweet cross,
to fix with a string a cross in the sky.

The white sand heats up
as one of us points out the snout of a pig
on the horizon, and higher up
a gaping alligator poised to eat a smaller cloud.

See how that one is a giant head,
like the devil wearing glasses
you say, but my eyes are shut against the sun
and I only hear your words,
softened and warped by the sea breeze,

telling me how the head is becoming a bicycle,
the high-wheel kind on playing cards,
while the sea rushes in, falls back—
marbles pouring endlessly onto a marble floor—

and the two of us so calm
it seems that this is not our only life,
just one in a series, charms on a bracelet,

as if every day we were not running
like the solitary runners on the beach
toward a darkness without shape
or waves, crosses or clouds,

as if one of us is not likely to get there first
leaving the other behind,
castaway on an island
with no pink houses or blue shutters,
no plum-colored ones trimmed in cream,
no offshore reef to burst the waves into foam,
and no familiar voice being bent in the wind.

Ignorance

It's only a cold, cloud-hooded weekday
in the middle of winter,
but I am sitting up in my body
like a man riding an elephant
draped with a carpet of red and gold,
his turban askew,
singing a song about the return of the cranes.

And I am inside my own head
like a tiny homunculus,
a creature so excited over his naked existence
that he scurries all day
from one eye socket to the other
just to see what scenes are unfolding before me,
what streets, what pastures.

And to think that just hours ago
I was as sour as Samuel Johnson
with a few bad sherries in him,
quarreling in a corner of the Rat and Parrot,
full of scorn for the impertinence of men,
the inconstancy of women.

And to think further that I have no idea
what might have uplifted me,
unless it was when I first opened
the front door to look at the sky
so extensive and burdened with snow,
or was it this morning
when I walked along the reservoir?

Was it when the dog
scared up some ducks off the water
and I stopped to watch them flapping low
over the frozen surface,
and I counted them in flight,
all seven—the leader and the six hurrying behind.

Death in New Orleans, a Romance

Long into the night my pencil
hurried across the page,
a young messenger boy
running his nervous little errands,
making lines,
making comparisons—
the world is like this, the moon like that,

the mind, I wrote, is like a wire birdcage
hanging from a stand
with a wooden perch and a tiny mirror,
home of a single canary,
I went on,
always the same one, the same song every day,
then quiet under the floral hood of night.

Always the same yellow and white feathers,
I continued,
yellow for the past, white for the future—
I added for symbolic weight—
and on the day I die,
I wrote, curving toward the elegiac,

the wire door will swing open
and the bird take flight,
looping over the ironwork of the city,
the water tanks and windowed buildings,
then up into the clouds and stars,
I typed,

leaving my body behind,
slumped upon a café table,
my empty head in a pool of wine,
the waiter and two customers
bending over me with obvious concern.

Air Piano

Now that all the twilight has seeped
out of the room
and I am alone listening,

the bass is beginning to sound
like my father
ascending the flights of stairs,

always the same cadence
every weekday evening,
a beat you could build a city on.

And the alto is the woman
I sat next to on a train
who wore a tiny silver watch around her wrist.

The drums are drops of water
on my forehead,
one for every inhabitant of China.

And the tenor, perhaps,
is someone's younger brother
who moved out west and never writes

or a swan passing under a willow.
But the piano—
the piano is the piano

you gave me one Christmas,
a big black curve
standing at the end of the room,

a red bow tied around its leg
while snow fell on the house
and the long rows of hemlocks.

Since then, I have learned some chords
and a few standards,
but I still love lying on the floor

like this, eyes closed,
hands locked behind my head,
laying down the solo on "Out of the Blue"

in the Fantasy Studios,
Berkeley, California,
on October 4th, 1951, when I was ten.

Drawing

Ink strokes on rice paper—
a wooden bridge
curved over a river,

mountains in the distance,
and in the foreground
a wind-blown tree.

I rotate the book on the table
so the tree
is leaning toward your village.

To My Patron

I do not require a ton of pink marble,
a hundred tubes of paint,
or an enormous skylit loft.

All I need is a pen,
a little blank notebook,
and a lamp with a seventy-five-watt bulb.

Of course, an oak desk would be nice,
maybe a chair of ergonomic design,
and a collie lying on an oval rug,
always ready to follow me anywhere
or just sniff my empty palm.

And I would not turn down a house
canopied by shade trees,
a swing suspended from a high limb,
flowering azaleas around the porch,
pink, red, and white.

I might as well add to the list
a constant supply of pills
that would allow me to stay awake all night
without blinking,

a cellar full of dusty bottles of Bordeaux,
a small radio—
nothing, I assure you, would go unappreciated.

Now if you wouldn't mind
leaving me alone—
and please close the door behind you
so there won't be such a draft
on my shoulders—
I will get back to work
on my long metrical poem,
the one I will recite to the cheering throng
prior to your impending beheading.

Writing in the Afterlife

I imagined the atmosphere would be clear,
shot with pristine light,
not this sulfurous haze,
the air ionized as before a thunderstorm.

Many have pictured a river here,
but no one mentioned all the boats,
their benches crowded with naked passengers,
each bent over a writing tablet.

I knew I would not always be a child
with a model train and a model tunnel,
and I knew I would not live forever,
jumping all day through the hoop of myself.

I had heard about the journey to the other side
and the clink of the final coin
in the leather purse of the man holding the oar,
but how could anyone have guessed

that as soon as we arrived
we would be asked to describe this place
and to include as much detail as possible—
not just the water, he insists,

rather the oily, fathomless, rat-happy water,
not simply the shackles, but the rusty,
iron, ankle-shredding shackles—
and that our next assignment would be

to jot down, off the tops of our heads,
our thoughts and feelings about being dead,
not really an assignment,
the man rotating the oar keeps telling us—

think of it more as an exercise, he groans,
think of writing as a process,
a never-ending, infernal process,
and now the boats have become jammed together,

bow against stern, stern locked to bow,
and not a thing is moving, only our diligent pens.

IV.

The Parade

How exhilarating it was to march
along the great boulevards
in the sunflash of trumpets
and under all the waving flags—
the flag of desire, the flag of ambition.

So many of us streaming along—
all of humanity, really—
moving in perfect sync,
yet each lost in the room of a private dream.

How stimulating the scenery of the world,
the rows of roadside trees,
the huge blue sheet of the sky.

How endless it seemed until we veered
off the broad turnpike
into a pasture of high grass,
heading toward the dizzying cliffs of mortality.

Generation after generation,
we shoulder forward
under the play of clouds
until we high-step off the sharp lip into space.

So I should not have to remind you
that little time is given here
to rest on a wayside bench,
to stop and bend to the wildflowers,
or to study a bird on a branch—

not when the young
keep shoving from behind,
not when the old are tugging us forward,
pulling on our arms with all their feeble strength.

The Only Day in Existence

The morning sun is so pale
I could be looking at a ghost
in the shape of a window,
a tall, rectangular spirit
peering down at me now in my bed,
about to demand that I avenge
the murder of my father.

But this light is only the first line
in the five-act play of this day—
the only day in existence—
or the opening chord of its long song,
or think of what is permeating
these thin bedroom curtains

as the beginning of a lecture
I must listen to until dark,
a curious student in a V-neck sweater,
angled into the wooden chair of his life,
ready with notebook and a chewed-up pencil,
quiet as a goldfish in winter,
serious as a compass at sea,
eager to absorb whatever lesson

this damp, overcast Tuesday
has to teach me,
here in the spacious classroom of the world
with its long walls of glass,
its heavy, low-hung ceiling.

No Time

In a rush this weekday morning,
I tap the horn as I speed past the cemetery
where my parents are buried
side by side under a smooth slab of granite.

Then, all day long, I think of him rising up
to give me that look
of knowing disapproval
while my mother calmly tells him to lie back down.

Balsa

A few days ago
when leaves were rushing by the windows,
I took this feeling
I have toward the world,
this mix of love and fear,
and carved a scale model of it
out of a block of balsa wood,
something you can find at any reputable hobby shop.

I used a set of knives
that would be very alarming horrifying shocking dreadful
in the hands of the wrong person,
especially if he had you strapped to a chair,
but in my hands, under a lamp,
they allowed me to express exactly
the way I feel toward people and things.

I did not smoke a cigarette while I worked
or sip a glass of ginger ale with ice,
as another might.
I just worked,
shaving away, like Michelangelo,
all the wood that was not my lust and apprehension.

When I had finished,
when I had gone as far as the knives
would allow me to go,
I placed my attitude toward the world
on a lace tablecloth,
a thing so light, so delicate and airy
I could think of nothing to do
but sit down in a chair and feel like
the happiest shell on the beach,
the happiest hobbyist in town.

Tomorrow I will get busy working
on another scale model,
this time of my childhood,
which I will fashion also from balsa,
being careful to keep the blades
from flying out of control
as they slice away at the soft cube of wood,
being careful not to draw any blood.

Then on Sunday, I will go to the park,
carrying the fragile thing under my arm,
and set it on the smooth surface of the oval pond.

And while the boys are sailing their boats,
running along the water's edge with their long sticks,
oblivious to the cries of their guardians,
I will stand off to the side
and watch my childhood—
that small vessel of wonder and cruelty—
being blown away by sudden unexpected gusts.

Elk River Falls

is where the Elk River falls
from a rocky and considerable height,
turning pale with trepidation at the lip
(it seemed from where I stood below)
before it is unbuckled from itself
and plummets, shredded, through the air
into the shadows of a frigid pool,
so calm around the edges, a place
for water to recover from the shock
of falling apart and coming back together
before it picks up its song again,
goes sliding around the massive rocks
and past some islands overgrown with weeds
then flattens out and slips around a bend
and continues on its winding course,
according to this camper's guide,
then joins the Clearwater at its northern fork,
which must in time find the sea
where this and every other stream
mistakes the monster for itself,
sings its name one final time
then feels the sudden sting of salt.

Earth

The sun is so clear and torch-like
on this cool October morning,
all I am aware of is the sensation
of its steady heat on my upturned face.

I am not thinking of how late the train is
that I am here to meet,
here with nothing to read, not even
the morning paper or a story by O. Henry.

The unfiltered burn of the autumn sun
on my skin is all that I know,
that and a small bubble of curiosity
about whether you could re-create this feeling in hell

if you managed to position yourself
just the right distance from the roaring
bank of furnaces where the sounds
of shoveling and howling are coming from.

But no, the damned would always be jostling
and pushing us closer to some fiery maw,
and in heaven the light would be
too hallowed, too theatrical to warm our faces.

And there would be no place for the train station
or the little café across the street,
no place in hell for the sunny table,
the bitter coffee, and the woman walking her dog.

Only the glare—I am imagining
with my eyes closed behind my favorite sunglasses—
the glare, some low chanting,
and the milling of some vast, incorporeal gang.

Colorado

Is there any part of the devil's body
that has not been used to name
some feature of the American topography,

I wondered when the guide directed
our attention to the rocky tip of a mesa
which was known as the Devil's Elbow.

He was a college student
just trying to do his summer job
and besides, the cumulus clouds

were massing beautifully
above the high rock face,
so I was not about to say anything,

but from my limited encounters
with evil, it looked to me more
like the hammer in the devil's inner ear.

Lying in Bed in the Dark,
I Silently Address the Birds of Arizona

Oh, birds of Arizona,

who woke me yesterday with your excited chirping,

where do you go to die?

So many of you, and yet never a trace

of your expirations,

no lump of feathers happened upon

here on the pavement

or another there on a square of lawn.

Are you down in the scrub turning in circles?

Do you tilt and fall on your side?

Do you lie there breathing among the warm rocks,

lie there breathing,

lie there

as the moon rises,

as the members of your flock fall silent for the night,

and the earth revolves around the center of your tiny eye?

Bodhidharma

This morning the surface of the wooded lake
is uncommonly smooth—absolute glass—
which must be the reason I am thinking
of Bodhidharma, the man who brought Buddhism
to China by crossing the water standing on a single reed.

What an absorbing story, especially
when you compare it to Zeus with his electric quiver
or Apollo who would just as soon
turn you into a willow tree as look at you sideways.

In every depiction, there is no mistaking
Bodhidharma, always up on his reed,
gliding toward the shores of China,

a large, fierce-looking man in a loincloth
delicately balanced on a little strip of bamboo,
a mere brushstroke on a painted scroll,
tiny surfboard bearing the lessons of the Buddha.

I recognized him one night in a Chinese restaurant
after the disappointment
of the fortune cookie, the dry orange, and the tepid tea.

He was hanging on a wall behind the cash register,
and when I quizzed the young cashier,
she looked back at the painting and said
she didn't know who it was but it looked like her boss.

Thinking of her and Bodhidharma
makes me want to do many things,
but mostly take off my shoes and socks
and slide over a surface of water on a fragile reed
heading toward the shore of a new country.

No message would be burning in my satchel,
but I might think of one on the way.
If not, I would announce to the millions
that it is foolish to invest too heavily
in the present moment,

not when we have the benefit of the past
with its great pillowed rooms of memory,
let alone the future,
that city of pyramids and spires,
and ten thousand bridges
suspended by webs of glistening wire.

Rain

It was raining all day in Kathmandu,
first a mist then a downpour,
but still, the wide street leading to the palace
was thick with people,
all waiting for the thumb of a delegate,
whose forehead had been smudged red
by the thumb of the king,
to smudge their foreheads red
on this, the holiest holy day of the year.

Only a few would receive the touch,
a merchant told me in his shop
as he rolled out rug upon rug—
hundreds of blinding stitches per square inch—
and another agreed as he opened
a folded sheet of paper and poured out
polished blue stones on a velvet cloth.

But still they waited, hunkered down
under flapping plastic and broken black umbrellas,
hoping to make a connection
the way one might hope to be connected
by a long chain of handshakes

to Babe Ruth or Alexander Pope
only without the need to stand
in a puddle all day soaked to the skin.

On the ride back to the hotel,
in the backseat of a taxi
I blackened one of my thumb pads
with a pen then pressed it to my forehead,
to show the world my belief
that even though we will all turn to ashes,
there may be an afterlife for some of us—
a realm of ink and wind-blown shelves,
a dominion of book spines and blown-out candles.

And that became the central tenet of the religion
I founded that day in a green
car driven by a suicidal Nepalese
in a bizarre hat with orange flowers around his neck.

The central and only tenet, I resolved,
as I looked out the rain-streaked windows
at the thin children,
the holy men shuffling along in their flip-flops,

carts piled with wet apples,

and on one sidewalk, groups of shiny wet ducks

huddled together in the rain,

presided over by men wagging long, pliant sticks.

Christmas Sparrow

The first thing I heard this morning
was a rapid flapping sound, soft, insistent—

wings against glass as it turned out
downstairs when I saw the small bird
rioting in the frame of a high window,
trying to hurl itself through
the enigma of glass into the spacious light.

Then a noise in the throat of the cat
who was hunkered on the rug
told me how the bird had gotten inside,
carried in the cold night
through the flap of a basement door,
and later released from the soft grip of teeth.

On a chair, I trapped its pulsations
in a shirt and got it to the door,
so weightless it seemed
to have vanished into the nest of cloth.

But outside, when I uncupped my hands,
it burst into its element,

dipping over the dormant garden
in a spasm of wingbeats
then disappeared over a row of tall hemlocks.

For the rest of the day,
I could feel its wild thrumming
against my palms as I wondered about
the hours it must have spent
pent in the shadows of that room,
hidden in the spiky branches
of our decorated tree, breathing there
among the metallic angels, ceramic apples, stars of yarn,
its eyes open, like mine as I lie in bed tonight
picturing this rare, lucky sparrow
tucked into a holly bush now,
a light snow tumbling through the windless dark.

The Stare

With a basin of warm water and a towel
I am shaving my father
late on a summer afternoon
as he sits in a chair in striped pajamas.

He screws up his face this way and that
to make way for the razor,
as someone passes with a tray,
as someone else sobs in a corner.

It is impossible to remember
such closeness,
impossible to know too
whether the object of his vivid staring is

the wavering treetops,
his pale reflection in the window,
or maybe just a splinter of light,
a pinpoint caught within the glass itself.

Surprise

This—
according to the voice on the radio,
the host of a classical music program no less—
this is the birthday of Vivaldi.

He would be 325 years old today,
quite bent over, I would imagine,
and not able to see much through his watery eyes.

Surely, he would be deaf by now,
the clothes flaking off him,
hair pitiably sparse.

But we would throw a party for him anyway,
a surprise party where everyone
would hide behind the furniture to listen

for the tap of his cane on the pavement
and the sound of his dry, persistent cough.

Poetry

Call it a field where the animals
who were forgotten by the Ark
come to graze under the evening clouds.

Or a cistern where the rain that fell
before history trickles over a concrete lip.

However you see it,
this is no place to set up
the three-legged easel of realism

or make a reader climb
over the many fences of a plot.

Let the portly novelist
with his noisy typewriter
describe the city where Francine was born,

how Albert read the paper on the train,
how curtains were blowing in the bedroom.

Let the playwright with her torn cardigan
and a dog curled on the rug
move the characters

from the wings to the stage
to face the many-eyed darkness of the house.

Poetry is no place for that.
We have enough to do
complaining about the price of tobacco,

passing the dripping ladle,
and singing songs to a bird in a cage.

We are busy doing nothing—
and all we need for that is an afternoon,
a rowboat under a blue sky,

and maybe a man fishing from a stone bridge,
or, better still, nobody on that bridge at all.

BILLY COLLINS is the author of six collections of poetry, including *Questions About Angels; The Art of Drowning; Picnic, Lightning;* and *Sailing Alone Around the Room: New and Selected Poems.* He is a Distinguished Professor of English at Lehman College of the City University of New York. He was appointed Poet Laureate of the United States for 2001–2003.

This book was set in Perpetua, a typeface designed by the English artist Eric Gill, and cut by the Monotype Corporation between 1928 and 1930. Perpetua is a contemporary face of original design, without any direct historical antecedents. The shapes of the roman letters are derived from the techniques of stone-cutting. The larger display sizes are extremely elegant and form a most distinguished series of inscriptional letters.